MASTIFFS

by Allan Morey

Content Consultant: Sarah K. Crain
Doctor of Veterinary Medicine
Tufts University
North Grafton, Massachusetts

CAPSTONE PRESS
a capstone imprint

Pebble Plus is published by Capstone Press,
1710 Roe Crest Drive, North Mankato, Minnesota 56003
www.mycapstone.com

Library of Congress Cataloging-in-Publication Data
Morey, Allan, author.
Mastiffs / by Allan Morey.
    pages cm. -- (Big dogs)
Summary: "Simple text and full-color photographs describe Mastiffs"--
Provided by publisher.
Includes bibliographical references and index.
ISBN 978-1-4914-7979-7 (library binding)
ISBN 978-1-4914-8563-7 (ebook PDF)
1. Mastiff--Juvenile literature. 2. Dog breeds--Juvenile literature.
I. Title.
SF429.M36M67 2016
636.73--dc23   2015030281

Editorial Credits
Nikki Bruno Clapper, editor; Juliette Peters, designer;
Morgan Walters, media researcher; Katy LaVigne, production specialist

Photo Credits
Corbis: 2/Jutta Klee/Ocean, 9; Glow Images: Deposit Photos, 17; Shutterstock: andrewvec,
(speedometer) cover, Ermolaev Alexander, 7, f8grapher, 19, Hywit Dimyadi, (dog silouette) cover,
Jaromir Chalabala, 13, Jaromir Chalabala, 21, kostolom3000, (dog head) backcover, 3, Mikhail
Olykainen, 15, Mikkel Bigandt, 5, Stephaniellen, (elephant) bottom right 22, Susan Schmitz, cover,
Reddogs, 11, Vitaly Titov & Maria Sidelnikova, 1, vlastas, (paw prints) design element throughout,
WilleeCole Photography, (dog) bottom left 22

Note to Parents and Teachers

The Big Dogs set supports national science standards related to life science. This book describes
and illustrates mastiffs. The images support early readers in understanding the text. The repetition
of words and phrases helps early readers learn new words. This book also introduces early readers
to subject-specific vocabulary words, which are defined in the Glossary section. Early readers
may need assistance to read some words and to use the Table of Contents, Glossary, Read More,
Internet Sites, Critical Thinking Using the Common Core, and Index sections of the book.

Printed in the United States of America in North Mankato, Minnesota.
102015   009221CGS16

Table of Contents

A TANK OF A DOG

Tank would be a perfect

name for an English mastiff.

Mastiffs are not just big.

They are muscular and

very strong.

Mastiffs were bred as
working dogs. People used
them to guard their homes.
Mastiffs are very loyal
and protective.

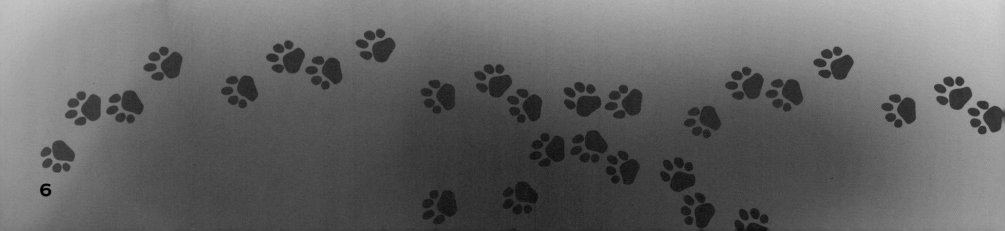

Mastiffs make great pets. They may be big, but they are also gentle. They are friendly with kids and smaller pets.

SOLID AND PROUD

Mastiffs are solid and heavy. They have wide heads and powerful chests. They look proud and eager.

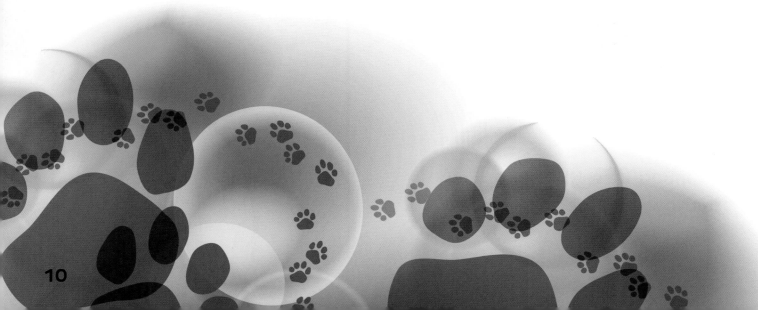

Mastiffs need to eat a lot
to get so big. They live for
seven to ten years, so food
costs add up!

CARING FOR A MASTIFF

All dogs need training. Mastiffs can take food off a table. They must learn not to step on small pets.

Mastiffs like furniture for people. Do you want to share your bed with a huge dog? Maybe not! Most mastiffs snore!

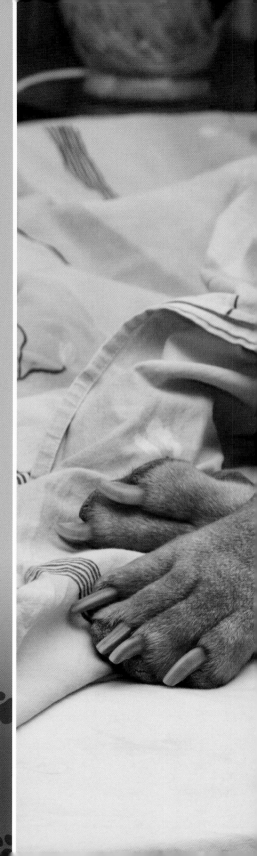

Mastiffs need a medium amount of exercise. They should take walks and play outside daily. Some mastiffs pull carts for exercise.

Mastiffs are calm, gentle, and loving. They have short coats, so they tend to be clean. How about that for a pet?

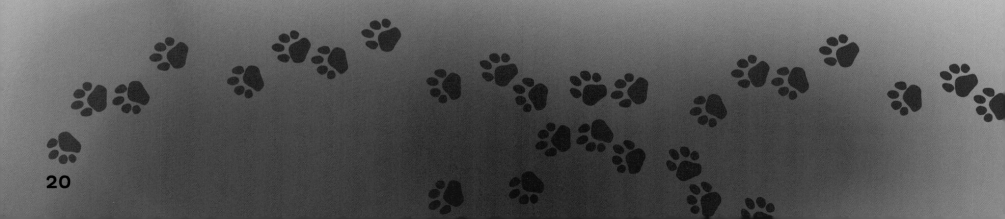

GLOSSARY

breed—to mate and produce young

coat—an animal's hair or fur

exercise—a physical activity done in order to stay healthy and fit

gentle—kind and calm

loyal—being true to something or someone

muscular—having lots of muscles

protective—wanting to keep someone or something safe

training—teaching an animal to do what you say

working dog—a dog that is bred to do a job, such as guarding homes or herding animals

HOW BIG ARE THEY?

	Mastiff	Baby Elephant
Average Height	27–33 inches (69–84 centimeters)	36 inches (91 cm)
Average Weight	120–230 pounds (54–104 kilograms)	200 pounds (91 kg)

42
36
30
24
18
12
6
0

READ MORE

Bluemel Oldfield, Dawn. *English Mastiff: The World's Heaviest Dog.* Even More Supersized! New York: Bearport Publishing, 2013.

Landau, Elaine. *Mastiffs Are the Best!* The Best Dogs Ever. Minneapolis: Lerner Pub. Co., 2011.

Nelson, Maria. *Mastiffs.* Great Big Dogs. New York: Gareth Stevens Pub., 2011.

INTERNET SITES

FactHound offers a safe, fun way to find Internet sites related to this book. All of the sites on FactHound have been researched by our staff.

Here's all you do:

Visit *www.facthound.com*

Type in this code: 9781491479797

 Check out projects, games and lots more at
www.capstonekids.com

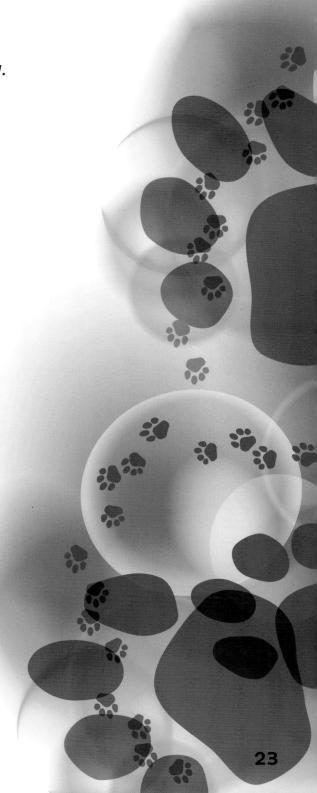

CRITICAL THINKING USING THE COMMON CORE

1. What does a mastiff look like?
   (Key Ideas and Details)

2. Many people want their pets to be good with children.
   Is a mastiff a good pet for children? Why or why not?
   (Integration of Knowledge and Ideas)

INDEX